JAN 1 2 2021
j581.4 K16p
Pretty tricky :the sneaky ways
p
K
D0383153

Written by ETTA KANER | Illustrated by ASHLEY BARRON
Pretty Tricky
THE SNEAKY WAYS PLANTS SURVIVE
OWLKIDS BOOKS

CONTENTS

For Lianna Simone, whose smile lights up my world

—E.K.

To Linda, for finding her green thumb

—A.B.

Text © 2020 Etta Kaner | Illustrations © 2020 Ashley Barron

All rights reserved. No part of this publication may be reproduced, stored in a retrieval system, or transmitted in any form or by any means, without the prior written permission of Owlkids Books Inc., or in the case of photocopying or other reprographic copying, a license from the Canadian Copyright Licensing Agency (Access Copyright). For an Access Copyright license, visit www.accesscopyright.ca or call toll-free to 1-800-893-5777.

Owlkids Books acknowledges the financial support of the Canada Council for the Arts, the Ontario Arts Council, the Government of Canada through the Canada Book Fund (CBF) and the Government of Ontario through the Ontario Creates Book Initiative for our publishing activities.

Published in Canada by Owlkids Books Inc., 1 Eglinton Avenue East, Toronto, ON M4P 3A1
Published in the US by Owlkids Books Inc., 1700 Fourth Street, Berkeley, CA 94710

Library of Congress Control Number: 2019956173

Library and Archives Canada Cataloguing in Publication

Title: Pretty tricky : the sneaky ways plants survive / written by Etta Kaner ; illustrated by Ashley Barron.
Names: Kaner, Etta, author. | Barron, Ashley, illustrator.
Description: Includes index.
Identifiers: Canadiana 20200152106 | ISBN 9781771473699 (hardcover)
Subjects: LCSH: Plant defenses—Juvenile literature. | LCSH: Plants—Adaptation—Juvenile literature.
Classification: LCC QK921 .K35 2020 | DDC j581.4/7—dc23

Edited by Stacey Roderick | Designed by Alisa Baldwin

Manufactured in Shenzhen, Guangdong, China, in April 2020, by WKT Co. Ltd.
Job #19CB2645

A B C D E F

ACKNOWLEDGMENTS: Much appreciation to Ian Baldwin for his information about hornworm caterpillars and to Stephen Skolnick for his help with how bladderworts function. Special thanks to my editor, Stacey Roderick, for her diligence, creativity, and good humor; to Alisa Baldwin for her clever design; and to Ashley Barron for her incredible illustrations, which make the book come alive!

INTRODUCTION

Have you ever thought of plants as sneaky or tricky? Probably not. But would you believe there are plants that trick insects into being their bodyguards? Or plants that are masters of disguise, or play sick to avoid being eaten? There are even some sneaky ones that do the eating themselves!

Why do plants need to be so tricky? For three reasons: to defend themselves, to get food, and to reproduce. In other words, their trickery is all about survival. Of course, plants don't actually think about being tricky. They don't have brains! But many scientists believe that plants adapt in ways that actually fool plants and animals (even the two-legged kind—humans).

As you read about the incredible adaptations in these pages, you'll realize there's a lot more going on with plants than you thought. Prepare to be surprised as you "leaf" through the pages of this book!

PLANTS ON THE DEFENSE

Plants have it tough. Animals eat them. People step on them. The sun beats down on them. Icy storms knock them around. Stuck there in the earth, plants have no way of defending themselves against these challenges.

Or do they?

Camouflage, bodyguards, playing dead—plants actually have plenty of clever self-defense tricks up their leaves.

A QUICK-CHANGE ARTIST

The Boquila vine grows in temperate rain forests, doing what vines usually do—reach for more light. The best way to do this? Climb a tree, of course.

What's unique about this vine is that as it grows and winds its way up toward the sunlight, its leaves change to match its host (the plant or tree it grows on). If the host tree's leaves are spiky, the vine's leaves become spiky. If the host tree's leaves are long, the vine's leaves grow long. The vine's leaves can also change their color and size. And when the vine travels over more than one type of tree, the leaves on each part of the vine match its own host.

Boquila vine

WHERE IT GROWS:
Chile and Argentina

Why does the Boquila vine do this? Scientists think it's a type of camouflage designed for protection. If a vine looks like the surrounding leaves, there's less chance it will catch the attention of a hungry herbivore (plant eater). How do Boquila vine leaves become copycats? Scientists are still trying to figure that out!

TRIPLE TRICKERY

If you were a wild tobacco plant and caterpillars were munching on your leaves, what would you do? You can't run away from those nasty predators, and you can't pick them off. But you *can* outsmart them!

The first thing newly hatched hornworm caterpillars eat are trichomes, hair-like growths on wild tobacco plants that are covered in a sweet, sticky substance. Eating the trichomes actually gives the caterpillars BO (body odor)! But to nearby predatory ants, that odor smells like takeout lunch. The ants scurry up the tobacco plant and carry the caterpillars back to their nests to feed to their own young.

Wild tobacco plant

WHERE IT GROWS:
Western Canada
and southwestern
United States

But if the hornworms manage to avoid being eaten and start feasting on a wild tobacco plant's leaves, the plant sends out a perfume that acts as an alarm. The smell attracts a natural enemy of hornworm caterpillars, big-eyed bugs, which rush to a tasty meal and the plant's rescue.

And if a tobacco plant is *still* being overrun by hornworm caterpillars, it has another tactic: it tricks the hawk moths, whose eggs hatch into the pesky hornworms. How? The plant changes the shape and smell of its flowers, so the moths look elsewhere for a place to land. Its flowers also begin to open in the morning instead of at night, when hawk moths normally dine on the nectar and lay their eggs.

PLAYING DEAD

Would you believe there's a plant that pretends to be dead?

Each leaf of the mimosa plant, also known as the sensitive plant, has a number of leaflets growing along its center stem. When an insect, animal, human, or even rain touches the leaflets, they fold together like hands in prayer. Often the whole leaf droops down, looking as if it has died. Then once the coast is clear, the leaflets slowly open up again.

Scientists believe this is the plant's defense mechanism. Insects that land on the leaflets may be startled by the sudden movement and make a fast exit. Also, herbivores may lose their appetite when they see the droopy, unappealing leaf. And then there are the razor-sharp thorns revealed along the stem when the leaflets fold up. They would make any animal want to avoid this plant!

Mimosa plant

WHERE IT GROWS:
South America, Central America, Africa, Southeast Asia, and Australia

One Australian scientist believes that the mimosa plant may also have a memory. Her experiment involved dropping the plants over and over again. At first, the leaflets folded, as expected. But after being dropped a number of times, the plants stopped folding their leaflets. They seemed to realize they weren't in danger after all. Even more amazing is that the same plants didn't react when the experiment was repeated a month later!

FAKING IT

Have you ever pretended to be hurt or sick to get out of doing something? These plants also use the "faking it" trick, but they do it for self-defense.

Some species of the passion flower vine need to defend themselves against female longwing butterflies. Longwings lay their eggs on this vine's leaves because it's the only plant that their hatched caterpillars can eat. But they won't lay eggs on leaves where there are already eggs. That's because they don't want the larvae (or young) of other insects to eat their eggs. They also want to make sure their young won't have to compete for food once they hatch. So the vine's leaves grow fake eggs—tiny spots that look just like longwing eggs! It's like putting up a sign that says, "Occupied! Lay your eggs elsewhere."

Passion flower vine

WHERE IT GROWS:
Colombia, Ecuador, Peru, Bolivia, and Brazil

The passion flower isn't the only plant that fakes it. Some caladium plants pretend to be damaged to avoid being eaten. They have variegated leaves—or green leaves with white patterns. These markings look like the trails left behind by leaf-mining larvae. When moths see the white trails, they assume larvae have already been there and eaten most of the leaves' nutrients, so they lay their eggs elsewhere.

GIVE AND TAKE

One look at the sharp thorns on this bull-horn acacia tree, and you know what its first line of defense is. But insects and climbing vines don't seem to feel threatened. So what's the tree's second line of defense? The acacia ant patrol!

If an insect lands on one of the acacia's leaves, the ants living on the tree sting the trespasser until it goes away. And if a vine winds its way up the trunk, the ants chew on it until it falls off the tree. The ants will also attack neighboring branches that touch the acacia, and plants that grow within a foot of the tree's base are soon goners, too.

Why are these ants such fierce defenders of a tree? The free room and board. The ants live inside the acacia's large hollow thorns. They also get to dine on sweet nectar and small, fatty beads that the tree produces especially for them. This give-and-take arrangement between the acacia and the ants is called symbiosis.

Bull-horn acacia tree

WHERE IT GROWS:
Mexico and parts of Central America

Tiny ants are able to deter the world's largest land mammals—African elephants—from eating Kenyan acacia trees!

MAKING MORE PLANTS

Many plants reproduce by making seeds that grow into new plants. But for flowering plants to make seeds, the flowers first need to be pollinated. Pollination happens when tiny grains of powder, called pollen, are moved from one flower to another of the same species. Most plants depend on animals and blowing wind to carry pollen for them. But in this chapter, you'll read about some tricksters that don't just wait for help to come!

KIDNAPPED!

You might be surprised to learn that this giant water lily is a kidnapper . . . well, beetle-napper.

When it first opens in the evening, the lily sends out a sweet perfume that lures scarab beetles into its center. Once the beetles are feasting on the sugar and starch they find there, the lily closes its white petals. The beetles are trapped! But they're not worried—there's plenty to eat and it's much warmer than outside. Besides, their captivity lasts only twenty-four hours. When the lily opens the next evening, the beetles, now covered with pollen, are free to fly to another giant water lily and pollinate it.

Strangely, after the beetles leave a pollinated flower, it turns from white to pink! Then it slowly sinks into the water, where it works on making a seed.

Giant water lily

WHERE IT GROWS:
Colombia, Peru, Brazil, and Bolivia

A giant water lily can be as wide as a large dinner plate!

MASTERFUL DECEPTIONS

Orchids may be beautiful, but they are also masters of deception. For instance, with its fringe of red hairs, metallic blue lip, and side lobes that resemble wings, the mirror orchid looks very much like a female scoliid wasp. And it smells like one, too! It sends out a chemical that tricks the male wasp into thinking the flower is a female wasp. When the male tries to mate with it, two of the orchid's pollen sacs become attached to the male wasp's head. Once he realizes he's been duped, he flies off to another orchid, where he will leave the pollen he just picked up.

Mirror orchid

WHERE IT GROWS:
Portugal, Spain, France, Italy, Switzerland, Bosnia, Croatia, Turkey, Syria, Morocco, Algeria, and Tunisia

Eastern marsh helleborine orchid

WHERE IT GROWS:
Cyprus and throughout the Middle East

The eastern marsh helleborine orchid has a different crafty trick. Its flower gives off chemicals that smell like the alarm signals emitted by aphids when they're in danger. When female hoverflies smell this scent, they rush to the orchid. Why? Hoverflies usually lay their eggs near aphids, which make perfect baby food for their newly hatched larvae. In the process of laying their eggs, the hoverflies pollinate the flower. When the larvae eventually hatch, there are no aphids to eat, and they die.

EXPLODING FLOWERS

Most plants open their flowers to attract pollinators. But not the scarlet mistletoe. Its summer blooms stay closed until they are opened with a "magic key."

The tui and the bellbird are the only types of birds that can "unlock" the flowers on these bushes. When looking for a ripe flower to open, these birds grab the flower bud in their beak and give it a sharp twist. The flower's petals instantly pop open … and surprise! The bird's feathers are showered with pollen. After enjoying the sweet nectar of one flower, the bird moves on to pop open another bud. Each flower it visits is pollinated with the pollen from the previous flower.

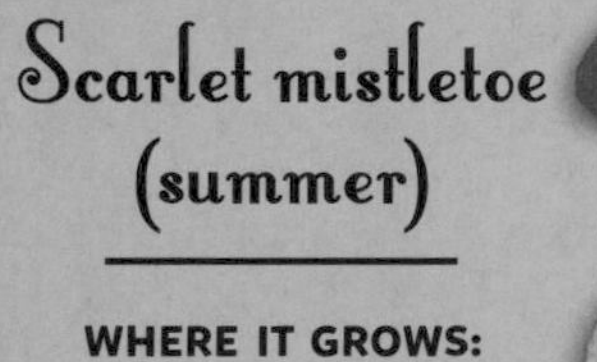

Scarlet mistletoe (summer)

WHERE IT GROWS:
New Zealand

Scarlet mistletoe (autumn)

WHERE IT GROWS:
New Zealand

Since these mistletoe shrubs grow high up on tree branches, they must take advantage of the birds to distribute their seeds. The birds are lured by the plants' pea-sized fruit, which they devour. When the seed of the fruit passes through the bird's gut, a hard outer coating comes off, leaving a sticky seed. When the bird poops, the undigested seed lands on a tree branch, where it stays stuck and starts life as a new plant.

WHAT IS THAT SMELL?

Warning! Do *not* try to sniff a starfish flower. Also known as the carrion flower, this plant smells like the rotting flesh of a dead animal! Not pleasant to humans, but to flies the smell is irresistible—like the perfect place to lay their eggs. Flies will deposit their eggs in poop or on carrion (decaying flesh), so their larvae will have plenty to eat when they hatch.

When a fly lands on a starfish flower, it finds leathery, hairy petals that feel like a dead animal's body and nectar that resembles the liquids from a decaying carcass. As the fly sips the nectar, it picks up pollen to carry to the next flower it visits. It also leaves its eggs behind, but the maggots that hatch will not survive. After all, there's no real rotten meat for them to eat.

Starfish flower

WHERE IT GROWS:
Throughout Southern Africa

The starfish flower is one of the largest in the plant world.

SEEDS IN DISGUISE

Dung beetles are duped not only into dispersing *Ceratocaryum argenteum* seeds, but into planting them, too!

The grass-like plant has large, hard seeds that look and smell a lot like the dung, or poop, of antelopes. And dung beetles love dung! They spend much of their time rolling balls of dung to a safe place, where they bury them to eat or lay their eggs in later. To an unsuspecting dung beetle, the seeds might seem perfect for this. Only later, when they try to eat the hard seeds or lay eggs in them, do the beetles realize that they've been cheated. Yet they just don't seem to learn. They keep rolling and burying those "dung balls"—all for the good of the plant.

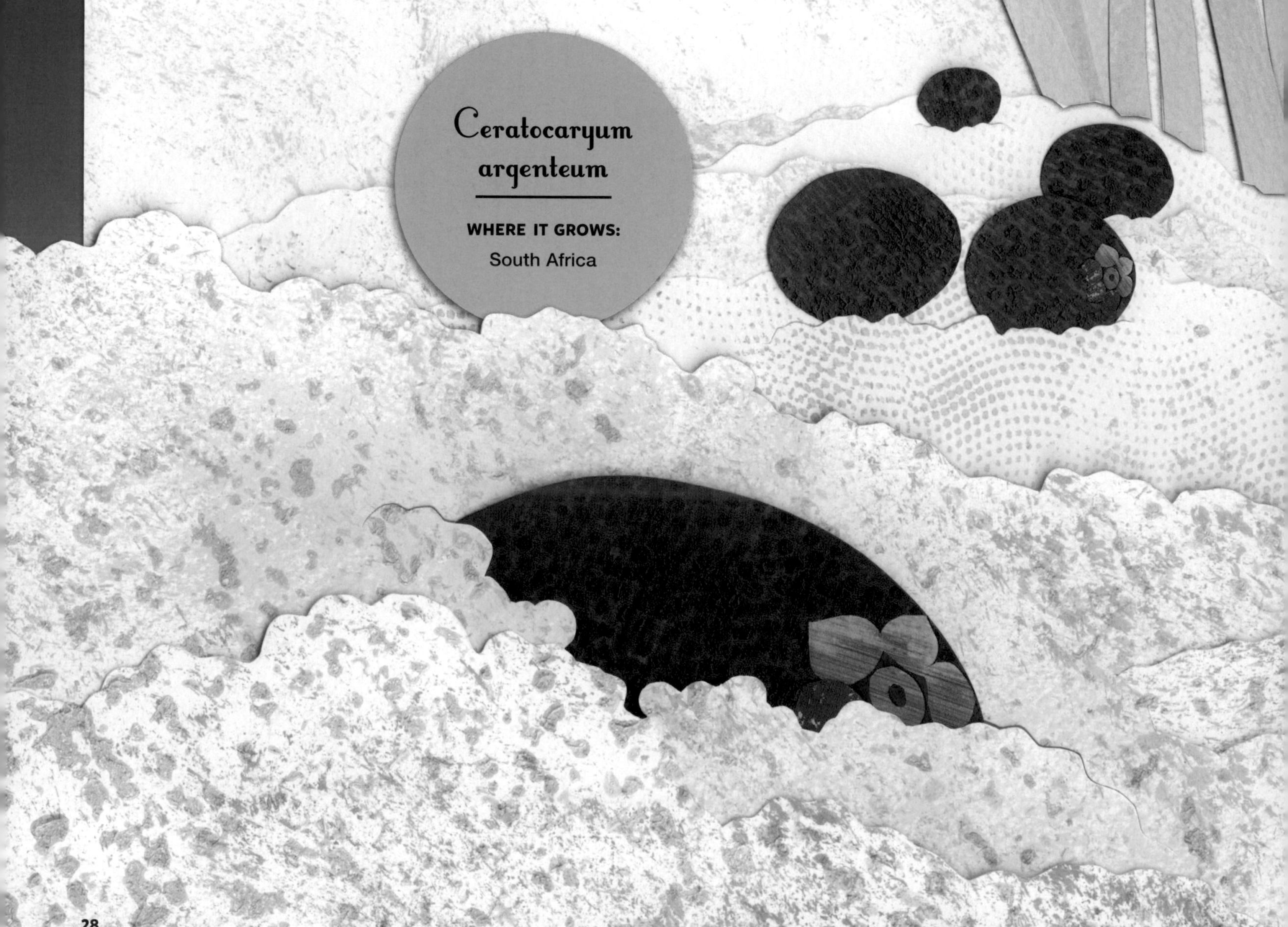

Ceratocaryum argenteum

WHERE IT GROWS:
South Africa

Dung beetles can roll dung balls that are fifty times their body weight—and do it upside down and backward!

SEED HITCHHIKERS

If you've ever walked along a riverbank or through a field, it's possible that a burdock plant has tricked you into dispersing its seeds. Burdock is a weed that grows spiny seedpods called burrs. Each burr contains twenty to forty seeds. When you brush against the plant, the burrs' tiny hooks stick to your clothes. Why do they do this? The burrs are hitching a ride away from their parent plant. When they eventually come off, they will hopefully land where their seeds can grow with less competition for nutrients, water, and light.

Burdock plant

WHERE IT GROWS:
Europe, Asia, North America, Greenland, and parts of South America and Africa

Thanks to burdock, we now have Velcro. Actually, it's really thanks to Swiss engineer George de Mestral, who got the idea for Velcro after trying to remove burdock burrs from his dog's fur.

Grapple plant

WHERE IT GROWS:
Parts of
Southern Africa

The grapple plant, also known as the devil's claw, is also a hitchhiker—but a much nastier one. Its seed case has twelve to sixteen "arms" with sharp hooked thorns that can become embedded in the soft flesh of grazing animals, crippling them. Luckily for the plant, it lives in the same ecosystem as elephants, rhinos, and ostriches. These animals have such tough feet that they can step on the spiny seed case without noticing and carry it for miles until it falls off.

NO CHEATERS ALLOWED!

Snapdragons are experts at outsmarting "cheater" insects—ones that are so small they can steal nectar from a flower without picking up pollen or leaving some behind. The plant just won't let these insects enter its flower! But for fat and fuzzy bumblebees, snapdragons put out the welcome mat.

Snapdragon

WHERE IT GROWS:
Parts of North, Central, and South America, Europe, Asia, and Africa

The snapdragon's welcome mat is its differently colored lower lip, which guides the bee to the flower's opening. Bumblebees are perfect for brushing against the snapdragon's anthers (the pollen-producing part of a flower). And what about those cheater insects? Lightweight insects don't have a chance! Only the weight of a bumblebee on the flower's lower lip can open the snapdragon's mouth.

FOOD, GLORIOUS FOOD!

Many plants make their own food. They use water and nutrients from the soil, carbon dioxide from the air, and sunlight. But several plants use trickery instead.

Some get insects to make food for them. For others, insects *are* their food. There's even a plant that steals food from other plants! Keep reading to find out more about some of the plant world's more surprising eating habits.

FOOD THIEF

The Western Australian Christmas tree gets its name because it blooms in December. Its flowers are a bright yellow-orange, and it can grow as tall as a three-story building. It is also very sneaky! The Christmas tree steals water and nutrients from the roots of other plants.

The victim can be nearby or as far away as the length of a football field. When its roots come into contact with another plant's roots, the Christmas tree first grows a small white ring around the neighbor root. Inside the ring, there is a blade that makes a cut into the neighbor. The Christmas tree's roots then enter the cut, and the tree absorbs any water and nutrients it finds there. This sneak attack helps the tree to survive the very dry summer months of southwestern Australia.

Western Australian Christmas tree

WHERE IT GROWS:
Southwestern Australia

It's not unusual for the roots of Western Australian Christmas trees to cut through underground telephone wires and other cables.

WITH A LITTLE HELP FROM MY FRIENDS

The Roridula plant has a problem. Even though its sticky leaves catch insects easily, the plant can't eat them. That's because it doesn't produce the enzymes needed to digest them. So Roridula has assassin bugs do the digesting for it. How? It invites the bugs to an all-you-can-eat buffet.

Roridula plant

WHERE IT GROWS:
South Africa

Assassin bugs are covered in a greasy substance that allows them to crawl all over Roridula leaves without getting stuck. Using their needle-like mouths, these bugs pierce other insects, such as flies, that have become stuck and inject them with a paralyzing poison. The poison also turns the insects' insides into a liquid for the assassin bugs to slurp up. After they have digested their meal, the assassin bugs deposit clear drops of feces on the Roridula leaves. The plant then absorbs the nutritious poop. Problem solved!

GOTCHA!

Picture this: you're walking down the street when suddenly you see a house made of colorful, shiny candy. Wouldn't you make a beeline toward it? That's what it's like when insects see a sundew plant. They simply can't resist the appeal of dewdrops glistening on the plant's tentacles like the sweetest nectar in the world.

But landing on those dewdrops is the start of the insect's worst nightmare. What looks like nectar is really a glue-like substance called mucilage. As the insect struggles to get free, more and more of the plant's sticky tentacles move in until it's covered in mucilage and can't breathe. (Some kinds of sundew plants even curl their leaves around their victim.) Once the insect is trapped, the tentacles produce enzymes to digest it.

Sundew plant

WHERE IT GROWS:
Eastern North America, parts of South America, and Europe

Venus flytrap

WHERE IT GROWS:
Eastern United States

The Venus flytrap is a cousin of the sundew plant. Insects are lured by the sweet-smelling nectar of its kidney-shaped leaves. The leaves are rimmed with stiff, comb-like bristles and have tiny touch-sensitive hairs on the inside surface. As an insect crawls around sipping nectar, it has no idea that by touching any two hairs, it will trigger the trap. Once triggered, the flytrap's leaves snap shut, forming a cage. A small insect might be able to escape between the bristles, but a larger one won't be so lucky. And as it struggles to break free, the leaves squeeze tighter, sealing the trap more firmly. Finally, the plant's digestive juices flow into the trap, drowning the insect.

PLANT OR TOILET?

You might already know that pitcher plants eat insects that have drowned in liquid at the bottom of their pitcher. But did you know that some species of this plant also depend on poop for nutrition? The *Nepenthes rajah*, one of the largest pitcher plants in the world, tricks tree shrews into using it as a toilet! How does it do that? The underside of the pitcher plant's lid-like leaf secretes nectar, which is a tasty treat for a tree shrew. To reach the sweet sap, the shrew perches on top of the opening of the pitcher, much like you sit on a toilet seat. As it licks up the sap, its poop falls into the pitcher below. The poop is the perfect fertilizer to help the plant grow in a habitat that doesn't have much nutrition in its soil.

Nepenthes rajah

WHERE IT GROWS:
Malaysian Borneo

Nepenthes rajah pitchers can hold as much liquid as a large milk carton.

SUPER SUCKERS

This bladderwort plant may be small, but it's also super sneaky and speedy. Found in lakes, streams, and waterlogged soils, the bladderwort has rootless floating stems with hundreds of tiny traps that suck in prey in less time than it takes to blink your eyes. Here's how.

Bladderwort plant

WHERE IT GROWS:
Worldwide, except Antarctica

Each trap is a tiny, hollow, balloon-like sac, or bladder, that pumps out water from its inside. At one end of the bladder is a trapdoor with tiny bristles and antennae that guide unsuspecting prey, such as water fleas, to it. When the prey touches a bristle, the door opens, and the victim, along with the surrounding water, is sucked into the trap. (Think of how water rushes into your mouth when you open it under water.) Then the trapdoor slams shut. About half an hour later, after the prey has been digested, the trap is ready for more action!

Some bladderwort traps are as small as the period at the end of this sentence.

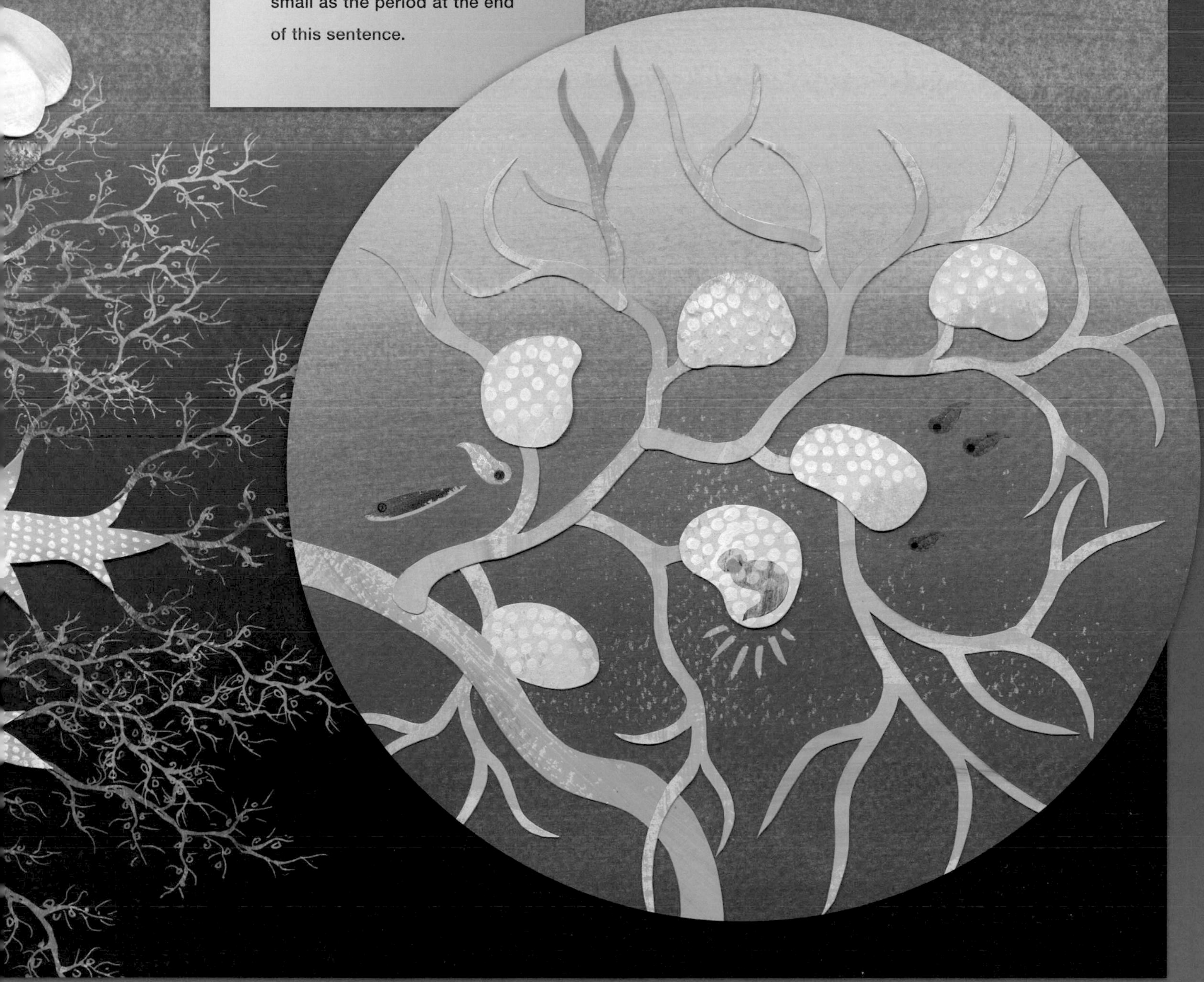

WANT TO KNOW MORE ABOUT PLANTS?

How Flowering Plants Make Seeds

Plants have many ways of reproducing. Flowering plants, such as giant water lilies and snapdragons, reproduce by making seeds.

To make a seed, a flower must be pollinated. Some flowers pollinate themselves, but others need pollen from another flower. When this is the case, here's what happens:

1. Pollinators (such as insects, birds, mammals, and the wind) pick up pollen from the anthers of one flower and move it to another flower.
2. The pollen is deposited on the sticky stigma.
3. A pollen grain sends a tiny tube down the style into the second flower's ovary. The tube contains a sperm cell that joins up with an egg in the ovary to grow a seed.
4. The seed is protected by a covering called a seed coat, which is sometimes surrounded by a fleshy layer that animals and people love to eat. (Think of fruits like cherries, plums, or peaches.)

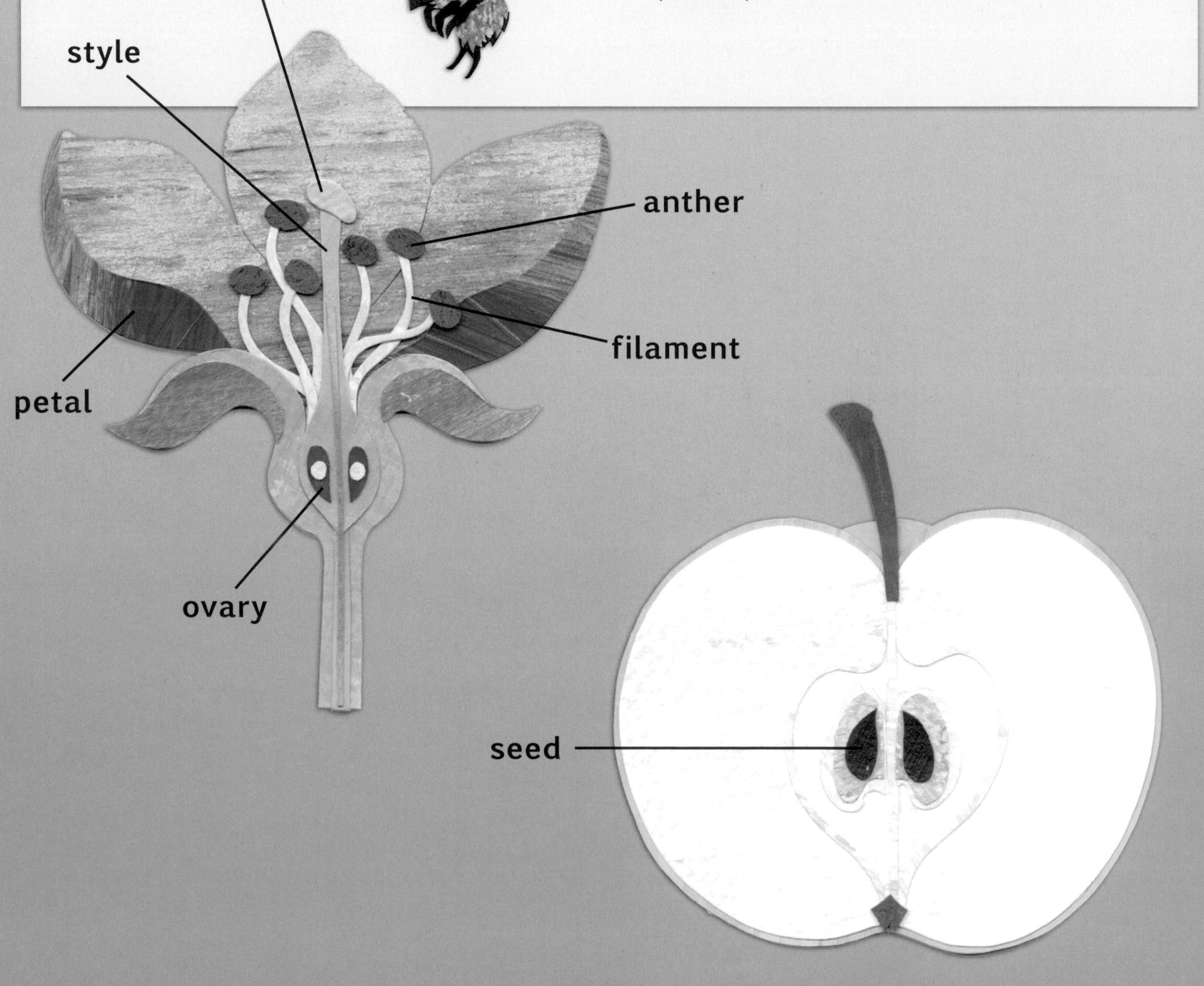

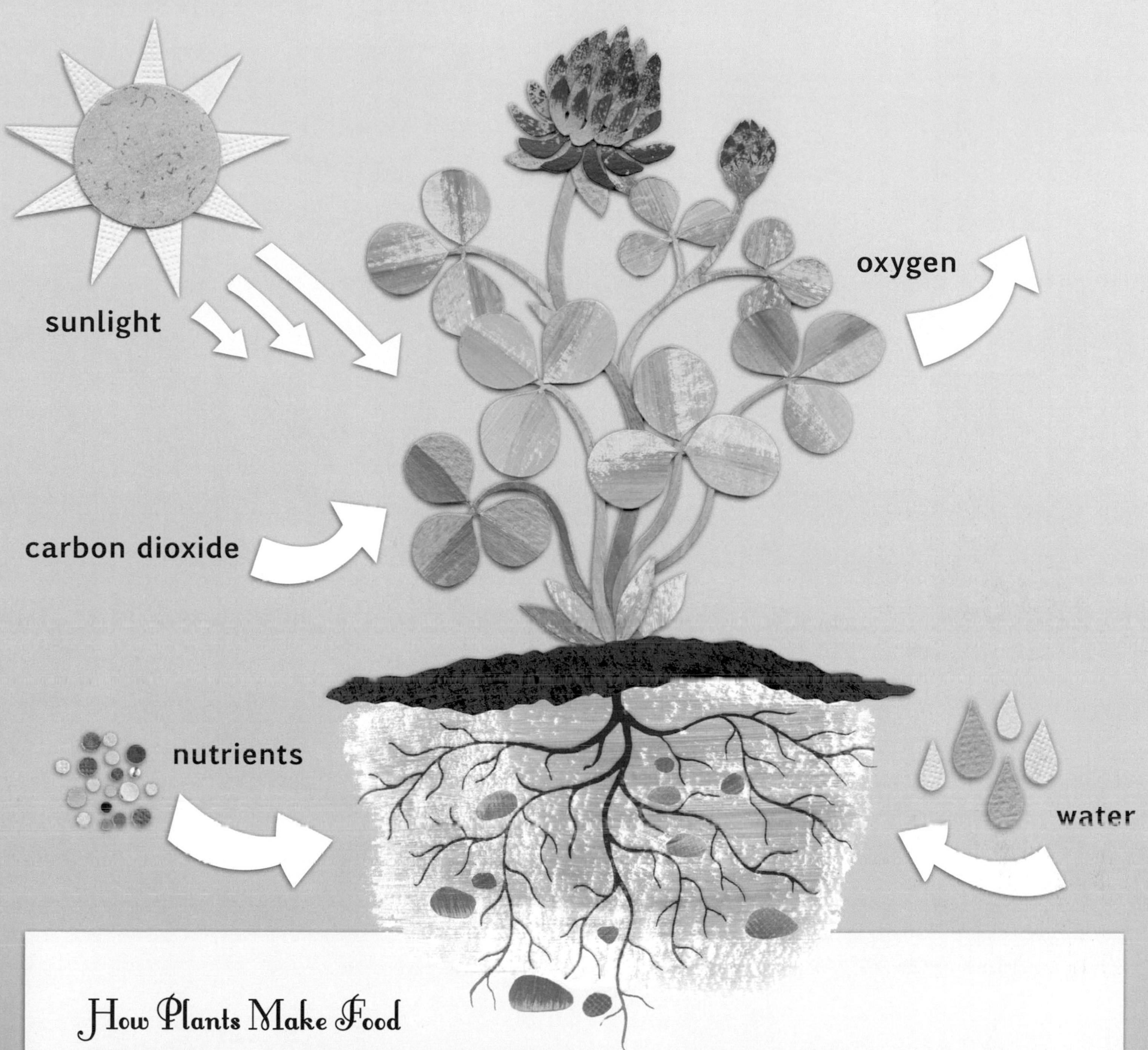

How Plants Make Food

Some plants, such as pitcher plants and sundews, get their nutrition from the insects they eat. But many other plants make their own food. This involves a number of ingredients and steps, just like a recipe in a cookbook. A recipe for a plant's food often looks like this:

INGREDIENTS

- water
- nutrients (found in the soil)
- carbon dioxide (a gas that's in the air)
- chloroplasts (parts in leaf cells that make them green)
- sunlight

1. The plant's roots suck up water mixed with nutrients from the ground. The water travels up the stem to the leaves.
2. Tiny holes in the plant's leaves (called stomata) absorb carbon dioxide from the air.
3. Chloroplasts in the leaves combine water, carbon dioxide, and energy from sunlight to make sugar and oxygen. The oxygen is released into the air, leaving behind the sugar, which is the plant's food. This process is called photosynthesis.

SOURCES

Index

Glossary

chloroplast: the part of a plant cell where photosynthesis takes place

ecosystem: the relationship all living things in a certain area have with each other and with their environment

enzyme: a substance that speeds up a chemical reaction

nutrient: a substance that living things absorb or eat to survive and thrive

ovary: the place in a flower where a seed forms

photosynthesis: the process by which a green plant uses energy from the sun to make its own food

pollen: tiny grains that help plants form seeds

stigma: the top part of the style where pollen sticks and germinates

stomata: tiny holes on plants through which water and gas pass

style: the stalk that connects the stigma with the ovary in a flower

symbiosis: a close relationship between two different species

Selected Sources

Attenborough, David. *The Private Life of Plants*. Princeton, NJ: Princeton University Press, 1995.

Chalker-Scott, Linda. *How Plants Work: The Science Behind the Amazing Things Plants Do*. Portland, OR: Timber Press, Inc., 2015.

Mabey, Richard. *The Cabaret of Plants*. New York, NY: W.W. Norton and Co., 2017.

Mellichamp, Larry and Paula Gross. *Bizarre Botanicals: How to Grow String-of-Hearts, Jack-in-the-Pulpit, Panda Ginger, and Other Weird and Wonderful Plants*. Portland, OR: Timber Press, Inc., 2010.

Plants of the World, Kew Science. Online.

Stevens, Martin. *Cheats and Deceits: How Animals and Plants Exploit and Mislead*. Oxford, UK: Oxford University Press, 2015.